I Am the Wind

Irish Poems for Children Everywhere

Edited by LUCINDA JACOB and SARAH WEBB

Illustrated by ASHWIN CHACKO

Little Island

I AM THE WIND:
IRISH POEMS FOR CHILDREN EVERYWHERE

First published in 2023 by Little Island Books,
7 Kenilworth Park, Dublin 6w, Ireland

First published in the USA in 2024

Designed and typeset by Niall McCormack
Project management and proofreading by Emma Dunne
Printed in Poland by L&C

Print ISBN: 978-1-915071-46-0

Little Island has received funding to support this book from the Arts Council of Ireland / An Chomhairle Ealaíon

10 9 8 7 6 5 4 3 2

To all those who helped me access books as a child and a teenager – novels, comics, poetry collections and art books: Mum, Dad, my grandparents, godparents, uncles, aunts, teachers, librarians, neighbours, parents' friends, pretty much the whole neighbourhood. What a life-changing gift! And thank you to my dear sisters, Kate and Emma, for letting me steal your books!
Sarah Webb

To Matthew, Sophie and Caroline. Also to Owen and my parents, especially my mum, who read and read to us as children and who passed on her love of poetry to me. To all my aunts, uncles and grandparents, for whom a birthday meant giving a book, and with it the joy of reading.
Lucinda Jacob

To Aaliyah, Liam and Kayden – may your world be ever filled with wonder and many books. To Bekki for always supporting me and encouraging me. To Amma and Appa for fostering my creativity and filling my childhood with the joy of books!
Ashwin Chacko

Contents

Introduction

We put this collection together because we LOVE poetry and we want to share this love with young readers. As the very first poem in this book so wonderfully puts it, a poem can open magical doorways. And a whole book of poems can open *multiple* doorways. Doorways to other worlds. Worlds of magic and adventure, warrior queens in training, night skateboarding ...

In these pages you will discover poems about hedgehogs and squirrels, whales and jellyfish, skipping and riding horses. You will read about friendship and loneliness, joy and sadness, conflict and feeling like an outsider. Some of the poems seem to speak to each other, so we put them side by side. Others are grouped by theme or tone. The poems are brought to life by Ashwin Chacko's lively and colourful illustrations.

You will find poems here by well-known poets like Eavan Boland and Seamus Heaney, and poems by newer poets like Polina Cosgrave and Chandrika Narayanan-Mohan. As well as choosing poems we already knew and loved, we wanted to include new poems, so we asked any writers who would like to be included to send us some poems too. We were delighted to find lots of talented new poets – and a big thank you to everyone who submitted their poems to us.

We have also created the *I Am the Wind* Poetry Kit, which you can get (free of charge) on littleisland.ie. This has lots of information about the poems in this book. It introduces readers to ways of writing that are used in some of the poems here, and it is chock-full of ideas to encourage young writers to try their hand at writing their own poems.

As E.R. Murray puts it in the opening poem of this collection: 'Let the journey begin.'

Lucinda Jacob and Sarah Webb

This Poem Can ...
E.R. MURRAY

This poem can ...
Open magical doorways
Pick a lock to your heart
Steal away on stormy seas
Make a dragon weep
Launch rockets to the moon
Offer somewhere to hide
Light a candle in the dark
Befriend a rainy day
Catch a slippery character
Awaken the explorer within
Be everything you wish for

Let the journey begin.

I Am from Ireland

ANONYMOUS

translated from the medieval English by Lucinda Jacob

I am from Ireland
the holy land
called Ireland.

Dear friend, please,
show your generosity,
come dance with me
in Ireland.

The Mystery

attributed to **AMERGIN GLÚINGEL**

translated from the medieval Irish by Douglas Hyde

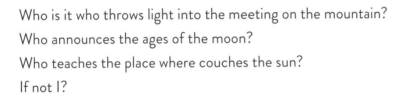

I am the wind which breathes upon the sea,
I am the wave of the ocean,
I am the murmur of the billows,
I am the ox of the seven combats,
I am the vulture upon the rocks,
I am a beam of the sun,
I am the fairest of plants,
I am the wild boar in valour,
I am a salmon in the water,
I am a lake in the plain,
I am a word of science,
I am the point of the lance in battle,
I am the god who creates in the head the fire.

Who is it who throws light into the meeting on the mountain?
Who announces the ages of the moon?
Who teaches the place where couches the sun?
If not I?

We Are

MICHELLE DUNNE

Fluent in nature-speak,
Hurricane and gentle breeze,
Hedgerow hunters,
Puddle jumpers,
Conker collectors,
Magic protectors,
Upturned faces,
Undone laces,
Blankets and books,
Ever-moving brooks,
Belly laughs,
Blurred photographs,
Moon gazers,
Trailblazers,
Chasing horses in sea foam,
Singing all the way home.

Snowdrops

KATIE DONOVAN

Snowdrops push
slim green helmets
through clogged leaves
and ragged nettles.
It took a while
for my addled eyes
to find their spears –
only when I turned away
an opalescent flash
pulled me back.

It's been a bit of a struggle
they seemed to say,
what with the rain,
the weeds, and all.
But we haven't given up
just yet.

Nightboarder

CHANDRIKA NARAYANAN-MOHAN

A boy skateboards in the rain
In the silence of a nightwet neighbourhood
His wheels protest against the pavement

As he passes under the window
He crescendos like a fighter jet
The roar echoing off the lightshut houses

And when he turns the corner
Only the sound of rain remains

Horse
CATHERINE ANN CULLEN

As he leaned from my saddle,
I heard something snap,
felt an instant of change.

Oisín was slow to notice,
but my hooves could feel the earth
pulse with voices of the dead.

He grew light as rain
and, out of the corner of my eye,
I saw him thin out like grey smoke,

Until there was nothing but
white bones resting by a boulder
in the shocked air.

Time had stood still
and now it galloped faster
than a fairy steed.

And even I, who have seen centuries pass
and sorceries flash without blinking,
took a minute to rear up

and away.

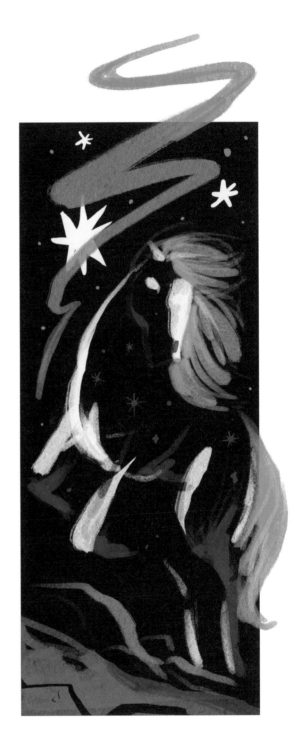

The Blackbird of Belfast Lough
CIARÁN CARSON

the little bird
that whistled shrill
from the nib of
its yellow bill:

a note let go
o'er Belfast Lough –
a blackbird from
a yellow whin

Int Én Bec
ANONYMOUS,
NINTH-CENTURY IRISH

Int én bec
ro léic feit
do rinn guip
glanbuidi

fo-ceird faíd
ós Loch Laíg
lon do chraíb
charnbuidi

The Blackbird of Belfast Lough
FRANK O'CONNOR

What little throat
Has framed that note?
What gold beak shot
    It far away?
A blackbird on
His leafy throne
Tossed it alone
    Across the bay.

On the Ning Nang Nong

SPIKE MILLIGAN

On the Ning Nang Nong
Where the Cows go Bong!
And the monkeys all say BOO!
There's a Nong Nang Ning
Where the trees go Ping!
And the tea pots jibber jabber joo.
On the Nong Ning Nang
All the mice go Clang
And you just can't catch 'em when they do!
So it's Ning Nang Nong
Cows go Bong!
Nong Nang Ning
Trees go ping
Nong Ning Nang
The mice go Clang
What a noisy place to belong
Is the Ning Nang Ning Nang Nong!!

Giraffe

AISLINN AND LARRY O'LOUGHLIN

'I wonder,' said the field mouse,
looking quite perplexed,
'why it is that all giraffes
have such enormous necks?'

'I know,' said the barn owl,
'at least I've heard it said,
it's because a giraffe's body
is so far from its head.'

Hedgehog

MOYA CANNON

It snuffles across the lawn at night,
a small, silver, trundling boar
with a long nose.

We are seldom quiet enough
to allow the moon to find
with whom we share our ground.

Leaf-Eater

THOMAS KINSELLA

On a shrub in the heart of the garden,
On an outer leaf, a grub twists
Half its body, a tendril,
This way and that in blind
Space: no leaf or twig
Anywhere in reach; then gropes
Back on itself and begins
To eat its own leaf.

To a Squirrel at Kyle-Na-No

W.B. YEATS

Come play with me;
Why should you run
Through the shaking tree
As though I'd a gun
To strike you dead?
When all I would do
Is to scratch your head
And let you go.

The Song of the Whale

LELAND BARDWELL

And the whale beached
In Lislarry. And they brought the JCB
And buried it. All thirty foot of it.
They said it was black,
Shining skin from the sea.
Grey blue, some argued
All thirty foot of it.
And the whale men came,
They came all the way from Cork,
For that is where the whale men
And the dolphin men hang out,
And they made their notes
And ecological plans and took
Blood samples and measured the tide
So that the whale now lies
Under the limestone reaches,
Proud steps to the summer storm,
Turquoise and shimmering,
Great sea mammal, partner of song.

The Great Blue Whale

KERRY HARDIE

Nobody knows
where he goes
nor what he does in the deeps,

nor why he sings,
like a bird without wings,
nor where he eats and sleeps.

The blue whale roves
through wintery groves,
his heart the size of a car,

his tongue, on the scale,
makes zoologists pale –
it's as heavy as elephants are.

A blue whale's vein
without stress or strain
could be swum down by you or me.

He's the biggest feature
that ever did creature
the sky, the land or the sea.

This Moment
EAVAN BOLAND

A neighbourhood.
At dusk.

Things are getting ready
to happen
out of sight.

Stars and moths.
And rinds slanting around fruit.

But not yet.

One tree is black.
One window is yellow as butter.

A woman leans down to catch a child
who has run into her arms
this moment.

Stars rise.
Moths flutter.
Apples sweeten in the dark.

Overconfident

MARIA QUIRKE

What's wrong with thinking I'm the centre of the universe?
Spin under the stars
wrapped in a patchwork quilt
and you'll see that you are too.

At Shankill Beach

MOYA CANNON

When a wave hauls back
it leaves its gleam in saturated sand
and, sudden, up from below, the lugworms
push the darkened sand in little coils and hills.

Where are they going in the dark,
working their tiny miracle,
turning plants into animals again,
eating their way blindly
through their known world?

from **A Skimming Stone, Lough Bray**

DAVID WHEATLEY

Skim a stone
across the lake surface,
marrying water and air:
turn this brick
of earth, while it flies,
from stone to living fire.

Metal Tide

POLINA COSGRAVE

My bedroom faces a supermarket
and every morning I wake up
from the noise the trolleys make
when pushed into each other
It's the sound of waves crashing on the beach
a silver sound of freshness
I open the curtains to watch
the ocean of trolleys rise

Scallywaggin'
RACHAEL HEGARTY

Between the Tolka and a disused quarry we learn
to cook a soup of puddle water and dandelions.
We brew it in a discarded tin of council paint
and stir it with windfall bits of twigs. Sticks

double as daggers. The longer ones are Finglas swords
pulled from the belt loops of corduroy scabbards.
Warrior Queens-in-training, we batter unseen enemies.

In Summer

GABRIEL FITZMAURICE

Just me and my friend Jessie
Sitting on the grass;
All the sun-long summer
We watch the world pass.

Just me and my friend Jessie
Sitting real slow
On the ditch outside our driveway
With the radio.

We listen to it sometimes
But mostly we just laze
And listen to the buzzing
And flutter of the days,

The lazy days, the hazy days
We hope will never end
Just sitting on the roadside,
Me and my best friend.

In summer.

Outside in Summer

LUCINDA JACOB

I hear other children
in other gardens, talking their games.
Shouts float over hedges and walls
and it feels like a secret;
I know them, they know my name
but don't know I'm here at all.

All afternoon, all day
I hope I'll hear the whump
of a too-hard kick and their ball
will land, softly thumping on our grass.
I'll throw it back
and they'll ask me to play.

Nearer Home

VONA GROARKE

My father is standing outside the front door,
pointing out to me the Plough and the North Star.
He says, 'Look up, child, just as far as you can.'
I see freckles join up on the back of his hand.

The Recipe for Happiness

GRACE WELLS

The recipe for happiness in our house
 is to take a cup of flour,
 and milk, two eggs, a pinch of salt,
 and whisk for half an hour.

Then take the creamy mixture
to the steaming frying pan,
ladle little circles in, as many as you can.

Watch them all turn gold and brown,
then sit down to eat,
sugar and
lemon on one side,
pour maple syrup to complete.

Friends

MONIKA NOWAKOWSKA

Hold my hand – I hear
A girl from my class saying next to me
I am a little scared – she knows
Hearing voices saying words I don't know
She holds my hand tightly
Smile is the only language I know

An Dráma Scoile
ÁINE NÍ GHLINN

Táim sa dráma scoile
Táimse i mo chrann
Bíonn orm mo ghéaga a luascadh
Anall agus anonn

Sa dráma anuraidh
Ba nóinín mé
Duilleoga is piotail
Ag rince sa ghaoth

An bhliain roimhe sin
Ba thonn mé cois trá
Is fuath liom drámaí scoile
An dtuigeann tú cén fáth?

School Play
ÁINE NÍ GHLINN

I'm in the school play
This year I'm a tree
I just wave my branches
Back and forth like this – See?

In last year's school play
I was a flower
Waving my leaves and petals
For the the best part of an hour

The year before that
I was a wave on the sea
School plays are boring
Don't you agree?

Pangur Bán

ANONYMOUS

translated from the ninth-century Irish by Robin Flower

I and Pangur Bán, my cat,
'Tis a like task we are at;
Hunting mice is his delight,
Hunting words I sit all night.

Better far than praise of men
'Tis to sit with book and pen;
Pangur bears me no ill-will,
He too plies his simple skill.

'Tis a merry thing to see
At our tasks how glad are we,
When at home we sit and find
Entertainment to our mind.

Oftentimes a mouse will stray
In the hero Pangur's way;
Oftentimes my keen thought set
Takes a meaning in its net.

'Gainst the wall he sets his eye
Full and fierce and sharp and sly;
'Gainst the wall of knowledge I
All my little wisdom try.

When a mouse darts from its den,
O how glad is Pangur then!
O what gladness do I prove
When I solve the doubts I love!

So in peace our tasks we ply,
Pangur Bán, my cat, and I;
In our arts we find our bliss,
I have mine and he has his.

Practice every day has made
Pangur perfect in his trade;
I get wisdom day and night
Turning darkness into light.

Ní Gá ...
GABRIEL ROSENSTOCK

ní gá ordú a thabhairt dó
níonn an cat
é féin

Without ...
GABRIEL ROSENSTOCK

without being told
to do so ...
the cat washes himself

Three Wishes

GERALDINE MITCHELL

I wish I was buzzing
with bees, a swarm
   in my hair, the fields
humming with blossom,
   honeyed song in the air.

I wish I was buzzing
with doorbells, friends
   calling; fizzing with current,
wires touching,
   sparks lighting the dark.

I wish I was buzzing
with secrets, bursting
   with things I can't tell,
huge smile on my lips,
   eyes on fire.

Smugairle Róin
RÉALTÁN NÍ LEANNÁIN

A leithéid d'ainm,
Dímheas i ngach siolla.
Bhí spórt ag an dream a chum an ceann sin.
Ach an neach iomlán grástúil
Ag snámh tríd na huiscí,
Beidh a díoltas aici
Leis an nimh san fheoil

Jellyfish (or Seal's Snot)
RÉALTÁN NÍ LEANNÁIN

Such a name
Contempt in every syllable
The people who made that one up, they had fun.
But that graceful creature
Swimming through the seas
She'll have her revenge
With poison in the flesh

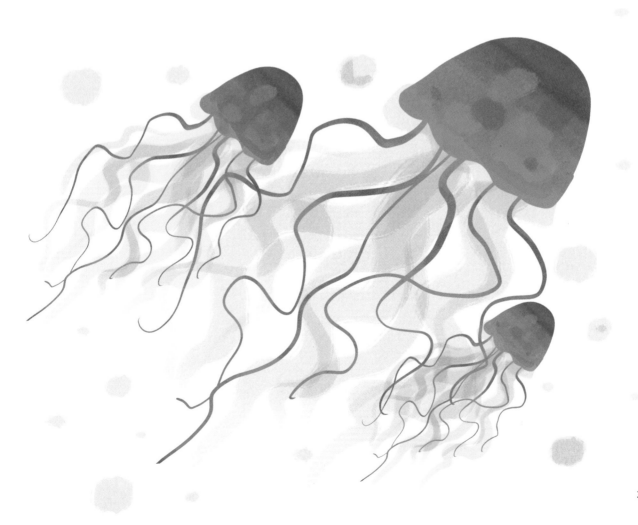

Earth Whispers

JULIE O'CALLAGHAN

White

when rain
whispers
it is snow

Green

when leaves
whisper
it is spring

Blue

when sky
whispers
it is wind

Grey

when cloud
whispers
it is wet

Red

when day
whispers
it is dusk

Purple

when hills
whisper
it is far

Yellow

when sun
whispers
it is heat

Black

when night
whispers
it is sleep

Summer Yearn

EITHNE HAND

It's almost dark in my bedroom,
outside the lake still glows.
If I could just slide from these covers
and lie in the tickling grass,
I'd eavesdrop on the crowd
readying for the night –
pulling on their fox trousers, badger coats,
heading for our neighbours' hills.
Hares on the beat, hedgehogs on the ball,
deer drinking long in the late night lake-bar.
Mink slink through brambles
as midnight's satin shifts from the east,
and a liquid dark slips over us all.

Praise

JANE CLARKE

Praise beetles in cow pats,
feasting like kings,

then rolling dung balls
into breeding chambers.

Praise woodlice bustling
through rotting leaves,

ants building
underground cities.

Praise the tunnelling
shoulders of moles

and earthworms ploughing
channels for rain.

Praise springtails,
bristletails and mites

that wait for the touch
of a burrowing root

to unleash
the sugars they crave,

then burst like joy
into multiplication.

Praise fungi
that bind and separate,

threading hyphae
through humus to create.

Blackberry-Picking

for Philip Hobsbaum

SEAMUS HEANEY

Late August, given heavy rain and sun
For a full week, the blackberries would ripen.
At first just one, a glossy purple clot
Among others, red, green, hard as a knot.
You ate the first one and its flesh was sweet
Like thickened wine: summer's blood was in it
Leaving stains upon the tongue and lust for
Picking. Then red ones inked up and that hunger
Sent us out with milk cans, pea tins, jam-pots
Where briars scratched and wet grass bleached our boots.
Round hayfields, cornfields and potato-drills
We trekked and picked until the cans were full,
Until the tinkling bottom had been covered
With green ones, and on top big dark blobs burned
Like a plate of eyes. Our hands were peppered
With thorn pricks, our palms sticky as Bluebeard's.

We hoarded the fresh berries in the byre.
But when the bath was filled we found a fur,
a rat-grey fungus, glutting on our cache.
The juice was stinking too. Once off the bush
The fruit fermented, the sweet flesh would turn sour.
I always felt like crying. It wasn't fair
That all the lovely canfuls smelt of rot.
Each year I hoped they'd keep, knew they would not.

Blackberry Feast

MARGOT BOSONNET

By the brambly hill where the blackberries cluster
The pond is an indigo-pink;
And the animals sigh at the lavender sky
As they lower their faces to drink.
All the frogs pickle purple from eating their fill,
For they guzzle and guzzle the berries that spill
In a knurly cascade to the foot of the hill,
Where they colour the water like ink.

Our Exercise for Today

PAT INGOLDSBY

Go and gallop on a wild horse
and hold onto its mane
and thunder down
the longest beach
in and out of the waves
in and out of the water.
Run into a forest
where you have never been
and crack the twigs
with your eager
frightened feet.
Catch a high branch
and swing on it.
Race down one side
of a mossy ditch
and up the other.
Whistle back at the birds
and chase a dizzy rabbit
round in circles.
Shout into a dark cave
and laugh at the echoes.
Look up at a clear bright moon
and wander around the heavens
with your eyes.
Race down a steep hill
until the headlong slope
makes you run
faster than you are able.

Stand so still
for so long
that all the voices
go away
and there is nothing left
to come between you
and the feel of who
you truly are
Now start again!

Finding My Space
CAROL BOLAND

I wish I could fly like a bird
        high up in an empty sky
higher and higher and higher still
        until I can be only me
where no one clips my wings
        and I have space to breathe.

Surnames

POLINA COSGRAVE

I'm a Russian girl with an Irish surname,
Who was a Russian girl with a Jewish surname,
Who was a Russian girl with a Russian surname
Who once spent nine months in the belly of
An Armenian girl with a Russian surname.
All these surnames
I can neither acknowledge or return,
each opening or eclipsing the other
like a Russian doll.

Leaving Gdańsk Główny

from The Weight of Water

SARAH CROSSAN

The wheels on the suitcase break
Before we've even left Gdańsk Główny.

Mama knocks them on some steps and
    Bang, crack, rattle –
        No more use.
          There are
            plastic bits
    Everywhere.

It's hard for Mama carrying a suitcase
And a bulging laundry bag.

It's hard for Mama
With everyone watching.

from **Maude, Enthralled**

for Maude Delap

DOIREANN NÍ GHRÍOFA

(i) Morning

Seventh of ten, little Maude is running
on Valentia strand again. In her braids,
sea wind unspins, until she skids. Sudden
in the sand, a jelly-bell, lump of glue-gunk
spiked with ink, tentacles spilling
from a fleshy pink, and oh! it stings.

(ii) Afternoon

The ocean alone.	Alone, the ocean.
And Maude, afloat.	Under her boat,
a world	of hover
and float,	of swim and flit
and gilled throats.	Maude peers
past ling	and dogfish,
past pollack	and conger eel,
until she sees	the tentacles
that she seeks.	All swell
and release,	those skewed
globules,	crimson- and
blue-streaked.	Maude considers
how each bell	draws up handfuls
of itself,	then lets go.
Maude learns	this lesson well;
Maude takes	notes.

The Jellyfish's Tongue Twister

GORDON SNELL

Jellyfish Bob
Is a wobbly blob
A wobbly blob is he.
He's a slobbery slob
With a gobbly gob
But Bob won't gobble ME!

Ar Iarraidh ...
GABRIEL ROSENSTOCK

AR IARRAIDH
ochtapas: má fheiceann tú é
glaoigh ar an Uisceadán!

Escaped ...
GABRIEL ROSENSTOCK

ESCAPED
octopus: if spotted,
ring Aquarium!

Worms Can't Fly
AISLINN AND LARRY O'LOUGHLIN

If worms can't fly,
then tell me please,
why do birds
wait in trees?

All the Dogs

MATTHEW SWEENEY

You should have seen him –
he stood in the park and whistled,
underneath an oak tree,
and all the dogs came bounding up
and sat around him,
keeping their big eyes on him,
tails going like pendulums.
And there was one cocker pup
Who went and licked his hand,
And a Labrador who whimpered
till the rest joined in.

Then he whistled a second time,
high-pitched as a stoat,
over all the shouted dog names
and whistles of owners,
till a flurry of paws
brought more dogs, panting,
as if they'd come miles,
and these two found space
on the flattened grass
to stare at the boy's
unmemorable face
which all the dogs found special.

An Old Woman of the Roads

PÁDRAIC COLUM

O, to have a little house!
To own the hearth and stool and all!
The heaped up sods upon the fire,
The pile of turf against the wall!

To have a clock with weights and chains
And pendulum swinging up and down!
A dresser filled with shining delph,
Speckled and white and blue and brown!

I could be busy all the day
Clearing and sweeping hearth and floor,
And fixing on their shelf again
My white and blue and speckled store!

I could be quiet there at night
Beside the fire and by myself,
Sure of a bed and loth to leave
The ticking clock and the shining delph!

Och! but I'm weary of mist and dark,
And roads where there's never a house nor bush,
And I am tired of bog and road,
And the crying wind and the lonesome hush!

And I am praying to God on high,
And I am praying Him night and day,
For a little house – a house of my own –
Out of the wind's and the rain's way.

Girl in a Rope
BRENDAN KENNELLY

By the still canal
She enters a slack rope,
Moves, slowly at first, round and round,
Gathering speed,
(Faster, faster now)
She clips the air without a sound –
Swift whirling sight,
Creator of a high design,
Orbiting in sheer delight
The red and white No Parking sign.

I'll Tell My Ma
TRADITIONAL

I'll tell my Ma, when I go home
The boys won't leave the girls alone,
They pulled my hair, they stole my comb
Well, that's alright, 'til I get home.

She is handsome, she is pretty,
She is the belle of Belfast city.
She is a-courting one, two, three
Please won't you tell me who is she?

Molly Malone

TRADITIONAL

In Dublin's fair city,
Where the girls are so pretty,
I first set my eyes on sweet Molly Malone,
As she wheeled her wheel-barrow,
Through streets broad and narrow,
Crying, 'Cockles and mussels, alive, alive, oh!'

'Alive, alive, oh. Alive, alive, oh,'
Crying, 'Cockles and mussels, alive, alive, oh.'

She was a fishmonger
But sure 'twas no wonder
For so were her father and mother before
And they each wheel'd their barrow,
Through streets broad and narrow,
Crying, 'Cockles and mussels, alive, alive, oh!'

She died of a fever,
And no one could save her,
And that was the end of sweet Molly Malone.
But her ghost wheels her barrow,
Through streets broad and narrow,
Crying, 'Cockles and mussels, alive, alive, oh!'

He Wishes for the Cloths of Heaven

W.B. YEATS

Had I the heaven's embroidered cloths,
Enwrought with golden and silver light,
The blue and the dim and the dark cloths
Of night and light and the half-light;
I would spread the cloths under your feet:
But I, being poor, have only my dreams;
I have spread my dreams under your feet;
Tread softly because you tread on my dreams.

March

FREDA LAUGHTON

Amid the taut gold wires of air the birds
Are feathered shuttles,
Weaving through a warp of twigs
A singing fabric.

Silver and black it is,
A plumed music,
Of thin ebony twigs
And birds' sequin voices.

Pumpkinhead

JULIE O'CALLAGHAN

If I stand at our fence
I can watch my brother
setting off for school.
It took him all last night
to carve the pumpkin on his head.
From here, he looks hilarious
with that huge orange head
and a flowing white sheet
covering the rest of him.
He carries his book bag
just like any other school day
and walks along humming,
up to the bus stop.
Will he sit on the bus
with a pumpkin on his head?
Yes, he will.
He'll live inside there all day –
He measured the grinning mouth
and it is big enough
to pass a spoon and fork
and candy bar into.
I lean over our fence
but he's just a little orange dot.

Hallowe'en

MICHAEL LONGLEY

It is Hallowe'en. Turnip Head
Will soon be given his face,
A slit, two triangles, a hole.
His brains litter the tabletop.
A candle stub will be his soul.

Visitor

NESSA O'MAHONY

A garden with a mouse in it
is a shape-shifting place;
a space of quick darts,
of dashes round plant pots,
courage snatched with birdseed.

It is a word hovering
out of reach, an image
half seen, a notion half-
realised, the perfect line
diffusing into vapour.

Symphony in Yellow
OSCAR WILDE

An omnibus across the bridge
Crawls like a yellow butterfly,
And, here and there, a passer-by
Shows like a little restless midge.

Big barges full of yellow hay
Are moored against the shadowy wharf,
And, like a yellow silken scarf,
The thick fog hangs along the quay.

The yellow leaves begin to fade
And flutter from the Temple elms,
And at my feet the pale green Thames
Lies like a rod of rippled jade.

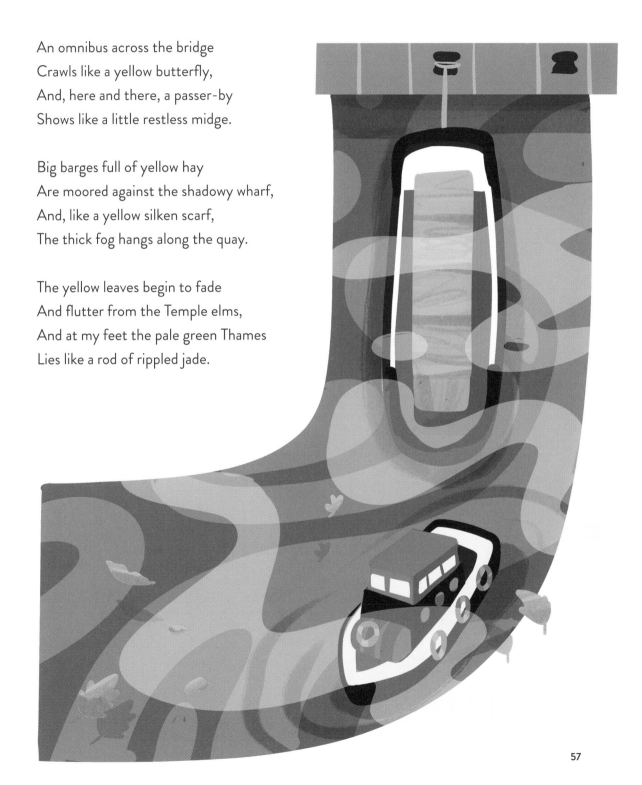

Ar Strae sa Chloigeann

MÁIRE ZEPF

Cá bhfuil mo bhróga scoile?
Bhí siad agam inné
Ach anois tá siad ar iarraidh
Anois tá siad ar strae

Chuardaigh mé faoin leaba
'is sa chófra ó bharr go bun
D'amharc mé sa chuisneoir
Ach faraor, ní raibh siad ann

B'fhéidir gur thit siad sa leithreas
'is d'imigh le sruth i gcéin
Nó gur sciobadh ag iolar san aer iad
Le go mbeadh siad anois mar nead éin

Caithfidh gur goideadh ag gadaí iad
Nó eachtrán ó Phláinéad Zúp Zalla
Mo léan, mo bhróga caillte
Fan nóiméad … cad é sin sa halla?

Astray in the Head

MÁIRE ZEPF

Where on earth are my school shoes?
I had them yesterday
But now they've disappeared
Now they've gone astray

I searched under my bed
And the cupboard under the stair
I even looked into the fridge
But sadly they weren't there

Maybe they fell down the toilet
And were flushed away to sea
Or were snatched by the claws of an eagle
To become a nest up a tree

They must have been stolen by robbers
Or aliens from Planet Zoop Zoll
Oh my poor departed school shoes
Hang on … what's that in the hall?

Little Jenny

GERRY HANBERRY

Little Jenny went to sleep
And woke up two feet taller.

Now the children in her class
Don't know what to call her.

The Wind That Shakes the Barley

KATHARINE TYNAN

There's music in my heart all day,
I hear it late and early,
It comes from fields are far away,
The wind that shakes the barley.

Above the uplands drenched with dew
The sky hangs soft and pearly,
An emerald world is listening to
The wind that shakes the barley.

Above the bluest mountain crest
The lark is singing rarely,
It rocks the singer into rest,
The wind that shakes the barley.

Oh, still through summers and through springs
It calls me late and early.
Come home, come home, come home, it sings,
The wind that shakes the barley.

A Vole Poem

LINDA McGRORY

A vole woke up one dreamy day and had a funny thought:
I am love, she said,
But with the letters jumbled up.
Look at me, a wee brown vole, so lowly, lowly in the ground,
Yet does it really matter where love is to be found?
I ran inside your shoe one day; you were a tad confused,

You thought I was a dormouse or perhaps a pygmy shrew.
But I am vole, a wee brown vole, a fact my friends all knew,
And with the letters jumbled up, I am love inside your shoe.

Pug
NICK LAIRD

Bruiser, batface, baby bear,
bounce in your moon suit
of apricot fur with some fluff
in your mouth or a twig or a feather.

Emperors bore you.

You with the prize-winning ears,
who grew from a glove
to a moccasin slipper
and have taken to secrecy

recently, worming in
under the furniture.
To discover you here
is to keep still and listen.

The settee begins wheezing.

WUFF

GABRIEL ROSENSTOCK

Dark ...
Dogs bark ...
I hear them howl,
Growl ...

WUFF!

What are they saying?
What are they baying?

Wuff! Wuff-wuff!

Wuff!

You'd think by now they'd had enough.

A Very Short Writing Course

PAT INGOLDSBY

Get a pen and a piece of paper and sit quietly.
Write down what it is that you want to say.
Write it down in the way you like to say it.
When you have done this you are finished.
Writing is as simple and uncomplicated as that.
Any second now a chorus of 'Ah yes buts'
will come rising up.
That is what makes it hard.

Taking My Pen for a Walk

JULIE O'CALLAGHAN

Tonight I took the leash off my pen.

At first it was frightened,

looked up at me with confused eyes, tongue panting.

Then I said, 'Go on, run away,'

and pushed its head.

Still it wasn't sure what I wanted;

it whimpered with its tail between its legs.

So I yelled, 'You're free, why don't you run –

you stupid pen, you should be glad.

Now get out of my sight.'

It took a few steps.

I stamped my foot and threw a stone.

Suddenly, it realised what I was saying

and began to run furiously away from me.

Dolphin
CATHERINE ANN CULLEN

Once, without warning,
you catapulted out of the water,
as though the sea
threw you to the sky,
and looked up laughing as you soared,
arms flung wide to catch you.

You were the sea's heart leaping from its chest,
or a memory of my father jumping,
thumping the air with happiness;
a rush of silver against the blue sky,
my heart leaping with you.

You carry our lost language,
the sounds we made before tongues
found the shapes of words.
Whistle to me, click your mouth
and I will answer.

In my dreams I am part of your mystery –
gliding underwater,
tuned to your echolocation:
a world champion synchronised swimmer,
an ocean trampoliner
bouncing into the sky.

from **The Deepest Breath**

MEG GREHAN

I know a lot
About me

There's only one thing
In the whole of me
That I don't know

It's something funny
It's in my chest
And sometimes my tummy
And always my head
It's a fuzzy feeling
Warm and squishy
And it makes me blush
And it only happens
When I look at my friend
Chloe

And I don't know what it is
Exactly

When Your Baby Sister Asks You if She's Pretty

NIKITA GILL

When your baby sister asks you if she's pretty, looking like the universe is weighing down her little bones with insecurity, resist the urge to say, 'Of course, darling. Of course you are.'

Tell her instead: 'Every day, I bless the stars that fell apart to allow your body's embers to glow to life.'

Tell her instead: 'In the seven billion people that exist on this planet you are the only one of your kind.'

Tell her instead: 'You are so much more than pretty. The stars that gave you to us made you to be like the sun. You are their best ever masterpiece. You aren't pretty. You are inspiring.'

Bird

LUCINDA JACOB

Sometimes being your best friend
Makes me feel like a little bird
With my beak stretched open
Ruffling my feathers,
Hungry.

Musha Mammy

CHRISSY WARD

Musha Mammy please don't send me to school,
Musha Mammy they treat me like a fool,
They stand around and call me names.

In this class I'm not the same,
Leave me at home, where I belong,
Not with these silly buffers, they're not my clan,
Leave me at home, where I belong.
I'll wash the dishes, I'll clean the floor, I'll mind the babies and a whole lot more.

In this horrible school they call me names,
In their hearts I'm not the same,
I'm only one Traveller among twenty-nine silly buffers,
They're not my kind.
Please let me home, where I belong,
I'm only one Traveller girl among twenty-nine.

Lá na bPeataí

ÁINE NÍ GHLINN

Ar Lá na bPeataí i Rang a Sé
d'ith piorána Eoghain
iasc órga Chathail.
Bhí Cathal trína chéile ar dtús.
Na deora ag titim go fras
nó go ndearna crogall Eleanóra
Cathal a shlogadh siar
in aon ailp mhór amháin.
B'in deireadh le deora Chathail.
Ach faraor b'in deireadh le Cathal freisin.

Pets' Day

ÁINE NÍ GHLINN

On Pets' Day in Year 6
Owen's piranha
swallowed Charlie's goldfish.
Charlie was quite upset.
He cried and he cried
until Eleanor's alligator
swallowed Charlie down
in just a single gulp.
That was the end of Charlie's tears.
Sadly, it was also the end of Charlie.

Puppy Love

ANNETTE REDDY

A rumbling – tumbling – scrumbling
Of feet and fur
And tiny teeth

A wriggling – squiggling – giggling
Of tails and
Sniffs and wigs and wags

A rambling – scrambling – brambling
Mess of
Bouncy – trouncy – flouncy
Bundle of joy
And fun
and yaps and yips
Hugs and nips

Puppies.

Irish Elk

CATHERINE PHIL MacCARTHY

Giant antlers shine at night
diamond, sapphire, branch

in a neighbour's garden, light
up the moonless dark

for children going to bed,
as if the Great Irish Elk,

extinct seven thousand years,
turned in his grave

beneath the lake at Lough Gur,
and bellowing rose

from the bog, trailing peat
from his hinds, to roam

the hills and woods of Ireland,
at this time of snow

falling all across the land,
on our road, ghost at

large, and twice as tall as Man
come back to haunt us.

What the Deer Said

MARK ROPER

I am my shyness, said the deer.
I am not searching for common ground.
I do not need to be cured.

What makes me tremble so?
The world's infinite sweetness,
sweetness by fear ripened.

Not our song but our silence
passes all understanding.
And we are silent when we sing.

If love can be a measure of distance
grant me that distance.
I am shyness. Love my shyness.

Stuff

DEREK MAHON

Woodshavings, oil and canvas, sand and stone,
atoms aswirl like barn dust in the sun,
already hold the paper, glass and artefacts
they're destined to become in a short while.
All that's required is skill, a sense of style
and a concrete devotion to the facts.

Stuff grows around us – jotter, ink, graphite –
with an interior life keen to create;
the picture above the table, the cracked plate,
broken specs, defaced books on the shelves
and the stuff dreams are made of, we ourselves
whose dancing atoms share a similar fate.

from **Stuck Indoors**

ENDA WYLEY

Rain all week
and the dog indoors
dry but discontented,
our sofa a ship of cushions,
newspapers, animal sighs –
the slow, dull hours
like crumbs, itchy on our skin.

And we are sailors
tossed this way and that
by winter's temper.
It breaks down doors,
sets house alarms wailing,
drenches passers-by
with the puddles of fury –

it even bullies the oak
that groans, bends, snaps –
and history crashes,
cracks the pavement,
sends shudders
like a tidal wave
rolling into our home.

The Sloth
ANNE McDONNELL

Even though the sloth
moves slow,
she gets to where
she wants to go.

The Sloth's Snooze
GORDON SNELL

The sloth is so lazy
He dozes all day
He thinks it is crazy
To go out and play.

He thinks it is crazy
To run, jump and crawl
The sloth is too lazy
To get up at all!

Tree Sloth

MARK GRANIER

Like trees, the tree sloth
knows something about growth

and time. With neither hands nor paws,
it hangs, upside-down, on clothes-hanger claws

and moves so very, very, very, very, very slow
that moss has time to grow

in its fur. When it comes to bath-
time, a tree sloth would murmur: 'I'll pass.'

One claw after another,
no hurry, easy does it, chill – the tree

sloth is the animal for me.

The Coal Jetty
SINÉAD MORRISSEY

Twice a day,
    whether I'm lucky enough
        to catch it or not,

the sea slides out
    as far as it can go
        and the shore coughs up

its crockery: rocks,
    mussel banks, beach glass,
        the horizontal chimney stacks

of sewer pipes,
    crab shells, bike spokes.
        As though a floating house

fell out of the clouds
    as it passed
        the city limits,

Belfast bricks, the kind
    that also built the factories
        and the gasworks,

litter the beach.
    Most of the landing jetty
        for coal's been washed

away by storms; what stands –
a section of platform
with sky on either side –

is home now to guillemots
and cormorants
who call up

the ghosts of nineteenth-
century hauliers
with their blackened

beaks and wings.
At the lowest ebb,
even the scum at the rim

of the waves
can't reach it.
We've been down here

before, after dinner,
picking our way
over mudflats and jellyfish

to the five spiked
hallways underneath,
spanned like a viaduct.

There's the stink
of rust and salt,
of cooped-up

water just released
to its wider element.
What's left is dark and quiet –

barnacles, bladderwrack,
brick – but book-ended
by light,

as when Dorothy
opens her dull
cabin door

and what happens outside is Technicolor.

My Ship
CHRISTY BROWN

When I was a lad my bed was the ship
that voyaged me far through the star-dusted night
to lands forever beyond the world's lip
dark burning olive lands of delight
across blood-red oceans under the stars
lorded by the scarlet splendour of Mars.

It is only a bed now spread with eiderdown
and the sheets merciless chains holding me down.

A Boy
MATTHEW SWEENEY

Half a mile from the sea,
in a house with a dozen bedrooms
he grew up. Who was he?
Oh, nobody much. A boy
with the usual likes
and more than a few dislikes.
Did he swim much? Nah,
that sea was the Atlantic
and out there is Iceland.
He kept his play inland
on an L-shaped football pitch
between the garage and the gate.
What did he eat?
Stuff his grandfather made,
home-made sausages,
potted pig's head.

He got the library keys
and carried eight books at a time
home, and read.
He read so much
he stayed in the book's world.
Wind rattled the window
of his third-storey room,
but his bed was warm.
And he stayed in his bed
half the day if he could,
reading by candlelight
when storms struck
and the electricity died.
How do I know all this?
You'd guess if you tried.

Exploring
MARGOT BOSONNET

When the tide has gone out
And the sand meets the sky,
We wander the sea-bed,
Jenny and I.

And paw-prints and foot-prints all mingle and mix
In erratic meanderings over the sand;
And we sink where it's yielding, and stamp very hard,
So the prints that we leave are impressively grand.

Further out on the shore, where the sand flows in ridges,
And hard corrugations bewilder the feet,
We gingerly tip-toe the puddle-logged valleys,
To search for the places the ridges all meet.

Then down to the cliffs that are twenty feet under
The highest of waters, we eagerly track;
Here are octopus holes all encrusted with barnacles
Under the curtains of thick bladderwrack.

And the carpets of seaweed are shifting and moving,
With rustling and crackling that makes Jenny bark;
There's a sea-arch where bootlaces hang like a beard,
And a long tunnel cave that's the home of a shark.

We search through the rock-pools of spiky anemones,
Foraging fingers, inquisitive paws,
Finding fissures of creatures, their tentacles waving,
And big hermit crabs with incredible claws.

Then up on the tideline we scavenge for shells:
Cockleshells, cowries, and pelican's feet,
Oystershells, razorshells, 'hear-the-sea' whelks,
And I fill my receptacle, fully replete.

When the tide's on the turn
And the sea meets the sky,
We journey on homewards,
Jenny and I.

Umbrella
RUTH ENNIS

I
Sometimes
Hold my umbrella
Upside-down to see just
How much water I can gather
From the crying skies but sometimes
It
Gets
Too
H   vy
ea

r
y   d
Me
Keep
To
And to protect me from the rain
Dumping all of this water out
To flip the umbrella back
Need a bit of help
Sometimes
I

A Bit of Free Verse

ALAN MURPHY

YIPPEE!

It's

such

a

PLEASURE

not

having

to

RHYME

the HOURS of the day after day after day

all

It

do

I'll   *Strawberries*   Hatstand

Think   Bed spring   **SAUSAGES**

I

Grandad   Penguins! Penguins! Penguins!

Grandad   YIPPEE!

Grandad

Grandad

Grandad

Grandad

Grandad

Grandad

Grandad

Grandad

Grandad   can't

ye

Bet   me   Bet

ye   catch

can't   can't

Catch   ye

me   Bet   can't   me   Bet

ye   catch

The Cat and the Moon

W.B. YEATS

The cat went here and there
And the moon spun round like a top,
And the nearest kin of the moon,
The creeping cat looked up.
Black Minnaloushe stared at the moon,
For, wander and wail as he would,
The pure cold light in the sky
Troubled his animal blood.
Minnaloushe runs in the grass
Lifting his delicate feet.
Do you dance, Minnaloushe, do you dance?
When two close kindred meet,
What better than call a dance?
Maybe the moon may learn,
Tired of that courtly fashion,
A new dance turn.
Minnaloushe creeps through the grass
From moonlit place to place,
The sacred moon overhead
Has taken a new phase.
Does Minnaloushe know that his pupils
Will pass from change to change,
And that from round to crescent,
From crescent to round they range?
Minnaloushe creeps through the grass
Alone, important and wise,
And lifts to the changing moon
His changing eyes.

On Finding a Dead Rat in the Living Room

PAUL Ó COLMÁIN

Alas, poor rat, you met your match.
You met our cat, he met his catch!

All Day I Hear the Noise of Waters

JAMES JOYCE

All day I hear the noise of waters
        Making moan,
Sad as the seabird is when going
        Forth alone,
He hears the winds cry to the waters'
        Monotone.

The grey winds, the cold winds are blowing
        Where I go.
I hear the noise of many waters
        Far below.
All day, all night, I hear them flowing
        To and fro.

from **A Calm**
ADELAIDE O'KEEFFE

How calm is the ocean,
　How soft the air round;
The ships have no motion,
　The waves have no sound:
All nature, as if it were sunk in fast sleep,
How clear the reflection of each in the deep.
　The hull, ropes, and mast,
　　At anchor safe ride;
Those fine vessels tall,
　　And high is the tide,
　　As they cover it wide:
Success to them all!

from **Moon-Light**
ADELAIDE O'KEEFFE

Silver moon pass not away
On the sea-wave dance and play
How we love to see thy light
Showing beauties to our sight.

The Four Honesties

DAVE LORDAN

The honesty of wind: everything must whistle by, everything must blow.

The honesty of sea: everything must churn, everything must flow.

The honesty of sun: everything must feed the fire, everything must glow.

The honesty of earth: everything must go to seed, everything must sow.

Ocean Song

E.R. MURRAY

Close your eyes
Still your breath
Can you hear
the ocean
singing?

Soft waves lapping barnacled rocks
Gushing, dancing, white horse froth
Rattle of pebbles dragged by the tide
Sudden splash of a gannet's deep dive
Ghostly tinkle of boat masts, breezy
Saltwater squeal of circling gull.

Hold a seashell
to your ear
Can you hear
the ocean
singing?

How will you reply?

My Best Friend's a Monster

NIGEL QUINLAN

My best friend's a monster
She has fangs and claws and teeth
We like to hang out together
Eating cookies and raw meat.
My best friend's a monster
I have pictures on my phone
I'm smiling, looking glam and fine
She's chewing on a bone.
My best friend's a monster
She hides beneath my bed
And when bad things come in my room
She claws them till they're dead.
My best friend's a monster
You better not mess with us
Because when it all gets too much for me
She'll pull out all your guts.

on o'connell bridge
RAFAEL MENDES

a seagull flies over a passerby
pounces
and gives a sausage roll
wings

Beans on Toast
ZAINAB BOLADALE

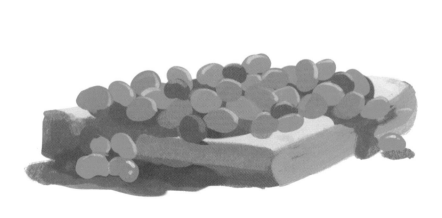

Beans on toast, beans on toast,
The sauce, a mystery, a secret almost.
I butter the bread, *click* goes the machine,
Now we wait for the toast to turn golden and sheen.
It's a humble dish, a simple pleasure,
Beans on toast ...
A national treasure!

Out and Back

LUCINDA JACOB

Open the front door and step through.
What's different? No sound of traffic.
Is that a robin singing?
A blackbird startles out of a hedge.
One car goes by.
Someone is coming towards us,
We cross the road,
They wave.
In our estate
People are in their front gardens,
Sitting or pottering about in the sun.
We turn for home.
Sitting or pottering about in the sun,
People are in their front gardens
In our estate.
They wave,
We cross the road.
Someone is coming towards us,
One car goes by.
A blackbird startles out of a hedge.
Is that a robin singing?
What's different? No sound of traffic
Open the front door and step through.

Everything Is Going to Be All Right

DEREK MAHON

How should I not be glad to contemplate
the clouds clearing beyond the dormer window
and a high tide reflected on the ceiling?
There will be dying, there will be dying,
but there is no need to go into that.
The poems flow from the hand unbidden
and the hidden source is the watchful heart.

The sun rises in spite of everything
and the far cities are beautiful and bright.
I lie here in a riot of sunlight
watching the day break and the clouds flying.
Everything is going to be all right.

Cat's Eye
DAVID BUTLER

City lights quiver like aspen leaves
in the slow liquorice river.
The wind has shivered a glass half-moon
into shimmering slivers,
into silver elver scribbling under where,
catlike, the Ha'penny Bridge
has over-arched its old arch-rival.

Merrion Square
JAMES STEPHENS

Grey clouds on the tinted sky,
A drifting moon, a quiet breeze
Drooping mournfully to cry
In the branches of the trees.

The crying wind, the sighing trees,
The ruffled stars, the darkness falling
Down the sky, and on the breeze
A belated linnet calling.

When You Walk

JAMES STEPHENS

When you walk in a field,
Look down
Lest you tramp
On a daisy's crown!

But in a city
Look always high,
And watch
The beautiful clouds go by!

Goat III
EVA BOURKE

The goat's favourite foods:
young leaves of the silver ash
the oak, birch and plantain
all types of ivy, sage, oregano
wild thyme and henbane
and every 30 days or so
it devours the whole moon.

Fox

LEANNE O'SULLIVAN

Halfway along the way a fox appeared
out of the perishing hedgerows and stopped
on the road in front of him,

the lines of her breast straight and clear,
fear having fallen away from there.
What is she doing? he thought. She said,

I am waiting to see what you will do next.
That's funny, he said, beginning to follow,
I am doing the very same thing.

And that was the way they went, morning
after morning, the hedgerows turning
their infinite colours, the body with its one fire.

I Like Being a Frog

SIAN QUILL

I like being a frog,
just so you know.
I enjoy my lilies and my pond,
and hopping to and fro.

Strange as it may seem,
I rarely long for a kiss.
I duck behind a reed
when I see a princess.

Yes, I'm a quiet sort of frog,
I never learnt to dance.
I like an early night, a good book.
I'm not cut out for romance.

I hope you find your prince
(or better, get a dog?).
Because I'm happy in my pond.
I like being a frog.

My Delicious Hat

PAUL TIMONEY

I had a hat made out of bread.
A seagull landed on my head.
He screamed 'caw caw' and pecked the peak,
Then flew off with it in his beak.

My gran tried shoes made out of lettuce.
A snail slid by and when he met us
He said, 'Fling floo' and chewed her toes.
Gran shrugged and sighed – 'That's how life goes.'

My dad wore trousers made of pollen.
A bee buzzed by – a bee named Colin.
He winked and grinned, said, 'Hello Sports,'
Next thing Dad knew – he's wearing shorts.

I Love These Hands

QUEVA ZHENG

I love these hands,
The hands of my grandparents.
These hands hold my hand,
While crossing the road.
These hands cook delicious foods,
When my brother and I are hungry.
These hands hold me up,
When I trip over.
These hands tie my hair up,
During the warm weather.
These hands wipe off my tears,
When I am sad.
These hands reach everything I want,
Everything that I cannot reach.
I love the wrinkles on these old hands.
One day they will be gone,
So I need to cherish these hands,
Until I cannot see or touch them,
Any more.

The Lion King

JOSEPH WOODS

You've been watching the weather
in your grandad's face
as he sleeps armchaired
in the sitting room

and how the newspaper flopped
to his feet like a seagull
big with wings of newsprint.

Watching the weather in his face
is more interesting than *The Lion King*
and when he wakes from his snooze
he always looks like a spaceman

landed on some strange planet
but still manages a smile
when you ask him, Grandad
were you old before you were old?

from **You Don't Know What War Is**

YEVA SKALIETSKA

7:50pm

It's very dark out. The darkest kind of dark. I feel too scared to go outside. Inna's friend has come over so we can all keep each other company.

We're not turning on the news because it just frightens us. I can still feel my heart beat anxiously but I'm trying to calm myself. With the heat from the little wood furnace, I'm feeling sleepier by the second.

Wake

CIARÁN CARSON

near dawn

boom

the window
trembled

bomb

I thought

then in
the lull

a blackbird
whistled in

a chink
of light

between
that world

and this

Winter in Inis Meáin

LOUISE C. CALLAGHAN

The immensity of sky,
its murmuring reflection
in flagstone pools.

No verticals to speak of,
only poles holding power-lines,
an occasional person

moving on the horizon.
The whole day
talks to me from the sky.

The Lake Isle of Innisfree

W.B. YEATS

I will arise and go now, and go to Innisfree,
And a small cabin build there, of clay and wattles made:
Nine bean-rows will I have there, a hive for the honey-bee;
And live alone in the bee-loud glade.

And I shall have some peace there, for peace comes dropping slow,
Dropping from the veils of the morning to where the cricket sings;
There midnight's all a glimmer, and noon a purple glow,
And evening full of the linnet's wings.

I will arise and go now, for always night and day
I hear lake water lapping with low sounds by the shore;
While I stand on the roadway, or on the pavements grey,
I hear it in the deep heart's core.

Changin Hosses

for my nephew Charlie

DAVE LORDAN

The first thing ya gotta do
is git offa the first hoss.

For a while, who knows how long,
ya no have a hoss.

Best not to lepp on the first hoss along.
Or the second, or the third ...

even if yer really browned off
and wantin quit to the next aisy option.

Aisy options always end ya up in the mud.
Ya know that. Don't forget it!

Git yerself a pretend hoss, if you must.
Let others believe it, not you.

Definitely don't take any hoss ya get offered.
That's tired riders tryin to get ridda
they hosses!

No, ya don't wanna git on any second-hand hoss
cast off by its previous rider.

Ya want a throwin hoss,
a hoss that keeps throwin.

The Pony's Eyes

TONY CURTIS

You see the bog
In greens and browns.

Ponies see it
In yellows and whites.

If ponies could paint,
The sky would be silver,

The sea a vivid red,
The islands blue.

Lakes would be golden.
Blackbirds would be yellow.

Think on it,
Then wonder no more

Why ponies always
Stand there looking amazed.

In a Dublin Museum

SHEILA WINGFIELD

No clue
About the use or name
Of these few Bronze Age things,
Rare
And in gold,
Too wide for finger-rings.
Till some old epic came
To light, which told
Of a king's
Daughter: how she slid them on to hold
The tail ends of her plaited hair.

The Standing Army

PAULA MEEHAN

Now that I carry my mother's spear,
wear my sister's gold ring in my ear,
I walk into the future, proud
to be ranked in the warrior caste,
come to play my part in defence
of my people, from my bed of wisdom sprung
to converse with the poets who
even now are flocking in the streets,
eyes aflame, weary of metrical talk,
starved of chant, craving tribal songs.

from **Ode**

ARTHUR O'SHAUGHNESSY

We are the music-makers,
And we are the dreamers of dreams,
Wandering by lone sea-breakers,
And sitting by desolate streams; –
World-losers and world-forsakers,
On whom the pale moon gleams:
Yet we are the movers and shakers
Of the world for ever, it seems.

93 Percent Stardust

NIKITA GILL

We have calcium in our bones,
iron in our veins,
carbon in our souls,
and nitrogen in our brains.
93 percent stardust,
with souls made of flames,
we are all just stars
that have people names.

Acknowledgements

This book was a real labour of love and we would like to thank all of those who helped us along the way. We want to thank everyone at Poetry Ireland, especially Jane O'Hanlon, Niamh O'Donnell, Paul Lenehan, Eoin Rogers, Elizabeth Mohen and Liz Kelly. It was so good of them to let us read our way through their brilliant library of contemporary Irish poetry.

Thank you to Orla Nic Aodha and all the staff of DCU Cregan Library. It was fantastic to be able to read their collection of Irish poetry books for children. A special thank you to Mary Shine Thompson, who welcomed us into her home and gave us the run of her great collection of poetry. We are particularly grateful as all these people made special efforts to allow us to read their books during the Covid lockdowns.

We would like to thank Children's Books Ireland for all their good counsel and to acknowledge all the help and support they give children's writers and illustrators.

And a great big thank you to our publishers, Little Island. Thank you to Matthew Parkinson-Bennett, Siobhán Parkinson, Elizabeth Goldrick, Kate McNamara and Emma Dunne. Thanks to Niall McCormack for design and layout. And, finally, a huge thank you to Ashwin Chacko, our wonderful illustrator, for bringing each page to life. It has been a pleasure working with you all!

Lucinda Jacob and Sarah Webb

Copyright Acknowledgements

The editors and publisher gratefully acknowledge permission to reprint the following poems in this book:
'The Song of the Whale' by LELAND BARDWELL from *The Noise of Masonry Settling* (2006), by kind permission of Dedalus Press. 'Beans on Toast' by ZAINAB BOLADALE by permission of the author. 'Finding My Space' by CAROL BOLAND by permission of the author. 'This Moment', from *In a Time of Violence* by EAVAN BOLAND. Copyright © 1994 by Eavan Boland. Used by permission of W. W. Norton & Company, Inc. Also from *Eavan Boland: New and Collected Poems* by permission of Carcanet Press Ltd. 'Blackberry Feast' and 'Exploring' by MARGOT BOSONNET from *Skyscraper Ted and Other Zany Verse*, Wolfhound (1994). by permission of the author. 'Goat III' by EVA BOURKE from *Spring in Henry Street* (1996), by kind permission of Dedalus Press. 'My Ship' from *Come Softly To My Wake* by CHRISTY BROWN. Published by Secker. Copyright © Christy Brown, 1987. Reprinted by permission of The Random House Group Limited. 'Cat's Eye' by DAVID BUTLER from *Liffey Sequence*, Doire Press (2021), by permission of the publisher. 'Winter in Inis Meáin' by LOUISE C. CALLAGHAN from *In the Ninth House*, Salmon Poetry (2010), by permission of the publisher. 'At Shankill Beach' and 'Hedgehog' by MOYA CANNON from *Collected Poems* by permission of Carcanet Press Ltd. 'The Blackbird of Belfast Lough' by CIARÁN CARSON by kind permission of the Author's Estate and the Susijn Agency. 'Wake' by CIARÁN CARSON by kind permission of the Author's Estate and The Gallery Press, Loughcrew, Oldcastle, County Meath, Ireland from *Collected Poems* (2008). Also from *Breaking News* (2003) by kind permission of Wake Forest University Press. 'Praise' by JANE CLARKE by permission of the author. 'Metal Tide' by POLINA COSGRAVE from *My Name Is Polina Cosgrave* (2020), by kind permission of Dedalus Press. 'Surnames' by POLINA COSGRAVE from *Writing Home: The New Irish Poets*, ed. Pat Boran and Chiamaka Enyi-Amadi (2019), by kind permission of Dedalus Press. 'Leaving Gdańsk Główny' by SARAH CROSSAN © Sarah Crossan, 2013, *The Weight of Water*, Bloomsbury Publishing Plc. 'Dolphin' and 'Horse' by CATHERINE ANN CULLEN by permission of the author. 'The Pony's Eyes' by TONY CURTIS from *Pony*, Occasional Press (2013) by permission of the author. 'Snowdrops' by KATIE DONOVAN from *Off Duty* (Bloodaxe Books, 2016). Reproduced with permission of Bloodaxe Books. 'We Are' by MICHELLE DUNNE by permission of the author. 'Umbrella' by RUTH ENNIS by permission of the author. 'In Summer' by GABRIEL FITZMAURICE from *I'm Proud to Be Me*, Mercier Press (2005), by permission of the author. 'When Your Baby Sister Asks You if She's Pretty' and '93 Percent Stardust' from *These Are the Words* by NIKITA GILL © Nikita Gill, 2022, published by Macmillan Children's Books, reproduced by kind permission by David Higham Associates. 'Tree Sloth' by MARK GRANIER by permission of the author. Extract from *The Deepest Breath* by MEG GREHAN, Little Island Books (2019) by permission of the author. 'Nearer Home' by VONA GROARKE by kind permission of the author's Estate and The Gallery Press, Loughcrew, Oldcastle, County Meath, Ireland, from *Other People's Houses* (1999). 'Little Jenny' by GERRY HANBERRY by permission of the author. 'Summer Yearn' by EITHNE HAND from *Fox Trousers*, Salmon Poetry (2020), by permission of the publisher. 'The Great Blue Whale' by KERRY HARDIE from *Something Beginning with P*, ed. Seamus Cashman, The O'Brien Press (2004), by permission of the author. 'Blackberry-Picking' from *Opened Ground: Selected Poems 1966-1996* by SEAMUS HEANEY. Copyright © 1998 by Seamus Heaney. Reprinted by permission of Farrar, Straus and Giroux. All Rights Reserved. Also from *100 Poems*, Faber and Faber Ltd. (2022) by permission of the publisher. 'Scallywaggin'' by RACHAEL HEGARTY from *Flight Paths over Finglas*, Salmon Poetry (2017), by permission of the publisher. 'A Very Short Writing Course' and 'Our Exercise for Today' by PAT INGOLDSBY from *Poems So Fresh and So New … Yahoo!*, Willow Books (1995), by permission of the author. 'Bird' and 'Outside in Summer' by LUCINDA JACOB from *Hopscotch in the Sky*, Little Island Books (2017) and 'Out and Back' by LUCINDA JACOB, Dun Laoghaire-Rathdown County Council Arts Office (2020), by permission of the author. 'Girl in a Rope' by BRENDAN KENNELLY from *Familiar Strangers: New & Selected Poems*

1960–2004 (Bloodaxe Books, 2004). Reproduced with permission of Bloodaxe Books. 'Leaf-Eater' by THOMAS KINSELLA from *Poems: 1956–1973*, Dolmen Press (1980), by kind permission of Sarah O'Malley. 'Pug', from *On Purpose* by NICK LAIRD. Copyright © 2008 by Nick Laird. Used by permission of W. W. Norton & Company, Inc. Also from *On Purpose*, Faber and Faber Ltd. (2007) by permission of the publisher. 'March' by FREDA LAUGHTON from *Poetry by Women in Ireland: A Critical Anthology 1870–1970*, Liverpool University Press, Copyright © 2012 Lucy Collins. Reproduced with permission of the Licensor through PLSclear. 'Hallowe'en' from *Collected Poems* by MICHAEL LONGLEY published by Jonathan Cape. Copyright © Michael Longley, 2006. Reprinted by permission of Penguin Books Limited. 'Changin Hosses' and 'The Four Honesties' by DAVE LORDAN by permission of the author. 'Irish Elk' by CATHERINE PHIL MACCARTHY from *The Invisible Threshold* (2012), by permission of Dedalus Press. 'Everything Is Going to Be All Right' and 'Stuff' by DEREK MAHON by kind permission of the author's Estate and The Gallery Press, Loughcrew, Oldcastle, County Meath, Ireland, from *The Poems: 1961–2020* (2021). 'The Sloth' by ANNE MCDONNELL from *The Caterpillar 19* (winter 2017), by permission of the author. 'A Vole Poem' by LINDA MCGRORY by permission of the author. 'The Standing Army' by PAULA MEEHAN by kind permission of Dedalus Press. 'on o'connell bridge' by RAFAEL MENDES from *Writing Home: The New Irish Poets*, ed. Pat Boran and Chiamaka Enyi-Amadi (2019), by kind permission of Dedalus Press. 'On the Ning Nang Nong' by SPIKE MILLIGAN © Spike Milligan Productions Limited 1959. 'Three Wishes' by GERALDINE MITCHELL by permission of the author. 'The Coal Jetty' by SINEAD MORRISSEY from *Parallax* (2013) by permission of Carcanet Press Ltd. 'A Bit of Free Verse' by ALAN MURPHY from *All Gums Blazing*, AvantCard Publications (2018), by permission of the author. 'Ocean Song' and 'This Poem Can …' by E.R. MURRAY by permission of the author. 'Nightboarder' by CHANDRIKA NARAYANAN-MOHAN by permission of the author. 'An Dráma Scoile'/'School Play' and 'Lá na bPeataí'/'Pet's Day' by ÁINE NÍ GHLINN from *Brionglóidí agus Aistir Eile*, Cló Mhaigh Eo (2008) and *Bronntanais agus Féiríní Eile*, Cló Mhaigh Eo (2010), by permission of the publisher. Extract from 'Maude, Enthralled' by DOIREANN NÍ GHRÍOFA from *To Star the Dark* (2021) by kind permission of Dedalus Press. 'Smugairle Róin'/'Jellyfish (or Seal's Snot)' by RÉALTÁN NÍ LEANNÁIN by permission of the author. 'Friends' by MONIKA NOWAKOWSKA by permission of the author. 'Pumpkinhead', 'Earth Whispers' and 'Taking My Pen for a Walk' by JULIE O'CALLAGHAN from *Tell Me This Is Normal: New & Selected Poems* (Bloodaxe Books, 2008). Reproduced with permission of Bloodaxe Books. 'On Finding a Dead Rat in the Living Room' by PAUL Ó COLMÁIN by permission of the author. 'The Blackbird of Belfast Lough' by FRANK O'CONNOR reprinted by permission of Peters, Fraser + Dunlop (www.petersfraserdunlop.com) on behalf of the Estate of Frank O'Connor. 'Giraffe' and 'Worms Can't Fly' by AISLINN AND LARRY O'LOUGHLIN from *Worms Can't Fly*, Wolfhound Press (2000), by permission of the authors. 'Visitor' by NESSA O'MAHONY from *Her Father's Daughter*, Salmon Poetry (2014), by permission of the publisher. 'Fox' by LEANNE O'SULLIVAN from *A Quarter of an Hour* (Bloodaxe Books, 2018). Reproduced with permission of Bloodaxe Books. 'I Like Being a Frog' by SIAN QUILL by permission of the author. 'My Best Friend's a Monster' by NIGEL QUINLAN by permission of the author. 'Overconfident' by MARIA QUIRKE by permission of the author. 'Puppy Love' by ANNETTE REDDY by permission of the author. 'What the Deer Said' by MARK ROPER from *Even So: New and Selected Poems* (2008), by kind permission of Dedalus Press. 'WUFF' by Gabriel Rosenstock from *Confessions of Henry Hooter the Third*, Brandon (1992), by permission of the author. 'Ar Iarraidh …'/'Escaped …' and 'Ní Gá …'/'Without …' by GABRIEL ROSENSTOCK by permission of the author. Extract from *You Don't Know What War Is* © YEVA SKALIETSKA, 2022, *You Don't Know What War Is: The Diary of a Young Girl From Ukraine*, Bloomsbury Publishing Plc. Also courtesy of Union Square & Co. 'The Sloth's Snooze' and 'The Jellyfish's Tongue Twister' by GORDON SNELL from *The Thursday Club: Animal Poems*, Dolphin (2000), by permission of the author. 'A Boy' and 'All the Dogs' by MATTHEW SWEENEY from *Up on the Roof*, Faber and Faber Ltd (2001) by permission of the publisher. 'My Delicious Hat' by PAUL TIMONEY by permission of the author. 'Musha Mammy' by CHRISSIE WARD from *Black Stones Around the Green Shamrock*, compiled by Michael O'Reilly and Máirín Kenny, Blackrock Teachers' Centre (1994), by permission of the author. 'The Recipe for Happiness' by GRACE WELLS by permission of the author. 'A Skimming Stone, Lough Bray' by DAVID WHEATLEY by kind permission of the author and The Gallery Press, Loughcrew, Oldcastle, County Meath, Ireland, from *Thirst* (1997). 'In a Dublin Museum' by SHEILA WINGFIELD from *Admissions*, Dolmen Press (1977), by permission of the author's estate. 'The Lion King' by JOSEPH WOODS from *Something Beginning with P*, ed. Seamus Cashman, The O'Brien Press (2004), by permission of the author. Extract from 'Stuck Indoors' by ENDA WYLEY from *Poems for Breakfast* (2004), by kind permission of Dedalus Press. 'Ar Strae sa Chloigeann'/'Astray in the Head' by MÁIRE ZEPF by permission of the author. 'I Love These Hands' by QUEVA ZHENG from *We Write What We Like*, by permission of the JCSP Demonstration Library Project.

About Lucinda Jacob

Lucinda Jacob is an Irish writer and librarian who writes poetry and stories for children. Her books include *Hopscotch in the Sky* (Little Island, illus. Lauren O'Neill), *Climate SOS!* and *Guzzler's Party* (Sustainable Energy Authority Ireland, illus. Alan Nolan). If she were a poem, she'd be rhythmical and song-like.

About Sarah Webb

Sarah Webb is an award-winning Irish children's writer, bookseller and champion of children's books. Her books include *Blazing a Trail: Irish Women Who Changed the World* (illus. Lauren O'Neill) and *A Sailor Went to Sea, Sea, Sea: Favourite Rhymes from an Irish Childhood* (illus. Steve McCarthy), both winners of Irish Book Awards. If she were a poem, she'd be free verse!

About Ashwin Chacko

Ashwin Chacko is an Indian-Irish author, illustrator and motivational speaker. He specialises in positively playful, visual storytelling to bring joy and encouragement. His mission is to champion creativity and empower people to find their inner spark through his art, books, talks and workshops. He has authored and illustrated several books including *Keep At It, Little Optimist, Everybody Feels Fear, A Little Book about Justice, What Wondrous Shapes We Are* and *Wild City*.